happiness is ...

happiness is ...

200 things I love about Dad

Lisa Swerling & Ralph Lazar

CHRONICLE BOOKS

SAN FRANCISCO

feeling safe when
you're around

being so excited to see you
when you get home

sitting down to a dad-tastic meal

laughing at your
old hairstyle

when you make
wishes come true

having you as my
fearless leader

your silly nicknames

your faith in my abilities

your magic touch

falling asleep on
your lap

your cute, slightly
old-fashioned ways

seeing you enjoy my
recommendations

your epic toasts

your bbq techniques

pancakes à la dad

when you spoil me

witnessing your
extraordinary talent
for napping

admiring your perseverance

when you trust me
behind the wheel

slipping you a
surprise

when you impress
my friends

a heart-to-heart
connection

when you give me just
the right advice

a card from you

heading off on a big road trip

being goofballs

working in unison

smoothing down
your facial hair

teaching you
something I learned

mutual admiration
and respect

your financial
support

when you love my friends

learning from your example

eating meals together

making you
proud

when you take
me shopping

having my own
private coach

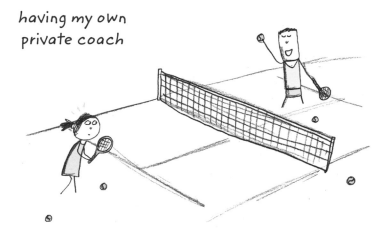

stealing your
cozy sweaters

watching you save the day

when you teach me cool things

dad wisdom

always being
a champion in
your eyes

teaching you to understand pop culture

knowing you'll catch me

your creative solutions

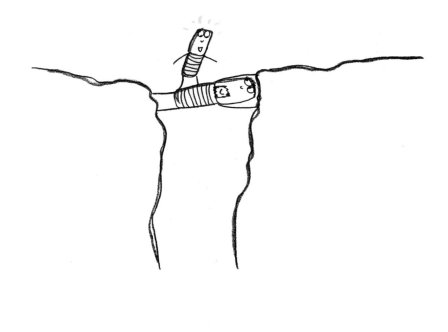

when amazing dads become
amazing grandpas

being a great team

feeling like a superhero

listening to your favorite music

a good game
of catch

doing chores together

when you accidentally say something
hilariously inappropriate

rocking out together

watching our favorite movies

having you on
speed dial in case
of emergency

being together for the holidays

corny dad jokes

making you smile

when you wipe
away the tears

seeing the world
with you

when you pick up all the essentials

cheering for
the same team

days out together

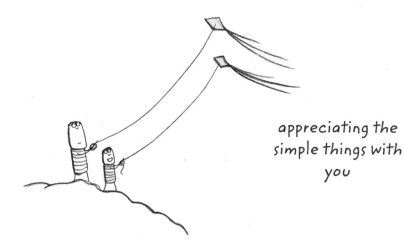

appreciating the
simple things with
you

piggyback rides

hearing you cheer me on

sharing your values

finding treats
that you bought
just for me

being your tech
support

making you laugh

taking care of you
for a change

feeling invincible by your side

showing my appreciation
for all you do for me

watching you
fix things

knowing "see you soon" means "I love you"

looking at old
vacation pictures

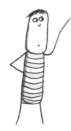

being allowed to make my
own mistakes

seeing myself in you

squeezing your hand
at my wedding

gaining your hard-won approval

hearing your voice on the end of the line

never letting life get
between us

precious everyday
moments

flying home to see you

your inimitable style

when you make
everything better

being inspired by
your example

when you sneak a treat into my bag

the smell of your
aftershave

surprising you with a cup of tea

tickle wars

seeing your "big softie"
side

having someone to
lean on

your unconditional love

when you pull out all the stops for a snack

a comfortable
silence

a deep bond of trust

getting help from a
patient teacher

being alike in all the best ways

our little adventures

our inside jokes

calling you with
important news

knowing you'll make time for me,
no matter how busy you are

realizing you kept all
the cards I made you

when you make
me feel special

appreciating down time

your patient explanations

being brought up by
a true original

your kindness

when you push me to do my best

imitating your
catchphrases

when we're all smiles

seeing you as a superhero

pranks that get
me every time

when I pick up the
check for a change

reminiscing over my
baby photos

when you spoil
me on sick days

knowing you're proud of my
accomplishments

shared
indulgences

when you let me win

coffee and a catch up

sharing once-in-a-lifetime experiences

when you inspire
me to live life to
the fullest

finding a box of my toys in your attic

growth and reflection

your tales that grow with the telling

a dad
wake-up
call

trying out your amazing dance moves

an early start with you

watching the master
chef at work

when you sing
songs from my
childhood

a helping hand

seeing my childhood art still on display

sharing
hobbies

a family trip

DEPARTURES

solving the world's
problems at dinner

takeout for dinner
when we're home alone

knowing what's
really important in life

when you surprise me with my
favorite things

feeling braver when
I'm with you

bringing out your
silly side

memories

when you meet me at the airport

exploring new places

treating ourselves

thinking of you

making your favorite drink
just the way you like it

being on the same
wavelength

a quick call
no matter the time

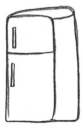

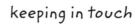

keeping in touch

knowing you're there for me
when I need you most

a special night out

showing you off to
my friends

moments of
tenderness

savoring the small things

building something together

seeing a framed photo
of me on your desk

knowing you love me through
the good and the bad

finding your gray
hairs

trying new foods
together

having special places
just for us

having a
safety net

having a whole conversation
with just one look

facing the world
together

knowing that you love
me for trying

recreating your
signature dishes

planning an
adventure

showing off
for you

hearing stories about
my childhood

celebrating special
occasions in style

our tv-watching marathons

finding my old school
photos tucked in your
drawer

hanging out in our pj's

feeling that you can protect
me from anything

hearing you tell that same story over and over again

making you a present

a family vacation with you
at the wheel

taking the
time to do
nothing at all

sharing your tears of joy

winning fair and
square

teasing you

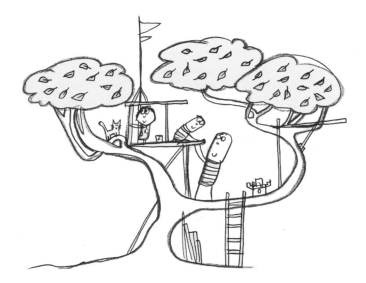

when you encourage
me to think big

quality time, just the two of us

stories that
stay with me

telling you all about my day

running errands together

when you act
like a kid

when you
introduce me
to new music

your unique
singing voice

knowing that you're a good person

when you put my needs
before your own

a shoulder to
cry on

the old-school
art of having fun

the relief of making up

realizing we've
become friends

ISBN 978-1-4521-4266-1
Manufactured in China.

Design by Lisa Swerling and Ralph Lazar

10 9 8 7 6 5 4 3 2 1

Chronicle Books LLC
680 Second Street
San Francisco, CA 94107
www.chroniclebooks.com